HEADStart

TUDORS
&
STUARTS

First published in Great Britain by
CAXTON EDITIONS
an imprint of
The Caxton Book Company,
16 Connaught Street,
Marble Arch, London, W2 2AF.

Copyright © 1998 CAXTON EDITIONS

ISBN 1 84067 029 0

A copy of the CIP data for this book is available from the British Library upon request.

With grateful thanks to Helen Courtney

Created and produced for Caxton Editions by
FLAME TREE PUBLISHING
a part of The Foundry Creative Media Company Ltd,
Crabtree Hall, Crabtree Lane,
Fulham, London, SW6 6TY.

Printed and bound in Singapore

HEADstart

TUDORS & STUARTS

Two Major British Dynasties Explained in Glorious Colour

MAUREEN HILL

CAXTON EDITIONS

Contents

Introduction: 1485-1714

The Tudor and Stuart periods of British history cover 223 years in which there were many difficult times for the rulers and the ordinary people. There were also many exciting times.

During this time England, Wales, Ireland and Scotland became united as one country. England, and eventually Britain, rose from being a small and unimportant European country to being one of the most powerful countries in the world.

This increase in power brought about wars with other countries in Europe. Within the country there was also a Civil War which led to the execution of King Charles I. For a short time after this, England did not have a monarchy at all and was ruled by Parliament instead. Later King Charles' son was crowned king.

There was a great deal of conflict within Britain caused by religion, sometimes between Catholics and Protestants but also between different groups of Protestants. Differences in religious beliefs were one of the causes of the Civil War.

It was also a time of discovery, both in science and in exploration. Some of the most famous plays ever written in English were performed in new theatres like The Globe. Sir Walter Raleigh, Sir Francis Drake and many other men explored sea routes around the world, travelling to places no one had ever seen before. They also set up trade with other countries and established new settlements. William Harvey discovered the way in which blood travels round the human body and Isaac Newton discovered the way in which gravity affects the Earth.

Henry VII

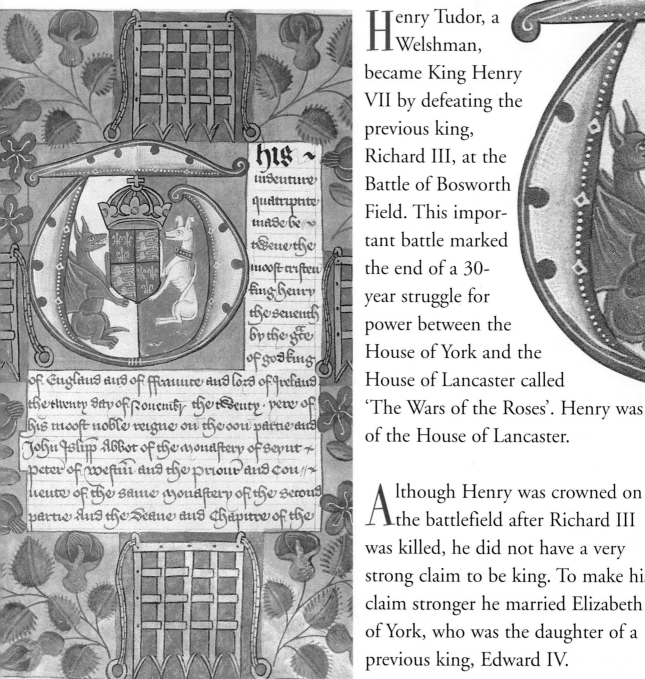

Henry Tudor, a Welshman, became King Henry VII by defeating the previous king, Richard III, at the Battle of Bosworth Field. This important battle marked the end of a 30-year struggle for power between the House of York and the House of Lancaster called 'The Wars of the Roses'. Henry was of the House of Lancaster.

Although Henry was crowned on the battlefield after Richard III was killed, he did not have a very strong claim to be king. To make his claim stronger he married Elizabeth of York, who was the daughter of a previous king, Edward IV.

The Earl of Warwick also had a strong claim to be king, so Henry locked him up in the Tower of London. Henry's enemies then put forward two 'pretenders to the throne'. One was a boy called Lambert Simnel who pretended to be the Earl of Warwick. He was captured and put to work in the royal kitchens. The other 'pretender' was Perkin Warbeck, who tried to invade England with support from France and Scotland. Warbeck was also caught and executed.

During his reign Henry became very rich. He did this by avoiding expensive wars with other countries and by taking control of the land that belonged to people who had supported his enemy, Richard III. He also made sure that all the taxes that were due to the king were paid.

Although he was disliked for making people pay taxes and high rents, most people respected Henry as a strong king who brought peace and prosperity to England.

Henry VIII and his Wives

Henry VIII was the king's second son and was not expected to become king. His older brother, Arthur, would have been king but he died before his father and Henry was next in line to the throne.

In all, Henry had six wives. The first of these was Katherine of Aragon, who had been married to Henry's brother, Arthur. Henry VII had wanted the marriage between Arthur and Katherine because it made a powerful friendship between England and Spain. So, when Arthur died, he persuaded the Pope to let Katherine marry Henry, even though the church disapproved of a woman marrying her dead husband's brother.

Katherine had many children but they all died, except one – Mary Tudor. When Katherine did not give him a son, Henry asked the Pope if he could divorce her so he could marry again. The Pope refused, so Henry

broke away from the Catholic Church and set up the Church of England. Henry was the head of the new Church, so he divorced Katherine and married Anne Boleyn.

This second marriage lasted four years. Like Katherine, Anne only produced a daughter, Elizabeth, and not the son Henry wanted. Anne was divorced and executed.

Henry's third marriage was to Jane Seymour. She had a son, Edward, and at last Henry was happy. Jane died 12 days after Edward was born.

Henry married three more times but had no more children. He divorced his fourth wife, Anne of Cleves, after only six months. He then married Katherine Howard, who was a lot younger than him. When she began to show an interest in other men, Henry became jealous and had her executed. His sixth and last wife, Katherine Parr, outlived him.

Life in a Tudor Town

Tudor society was organized into four main classes of people. Most of the population were peasants who lived in the countryside. They were very poor and belonged to the 'labouring classes'. The next class up were the yeomen, who usually ran small farms. Then came the merchants and crafts-men who made money by working and trading in the towns. Above them were the nobles, wealthy people and senior churchmen. Many people from this class were involved in the government of the country.

People who lived in towns were usually involved with making things or with trade. Wool was a very important product and the process of making wool into cloth was one of the jobs of the craft people who lived in the towns. New machines like the spinning wheel helped in this process. Towns like Manchester became important centres of the cloth industry.

Coastal towns such as Liverpool, Bristol and London also became very important centres of trade. From them England could trade goods with the rest of Europe, Russia, India, North Africa and the new settlements in the Americas.

The towns were very busy and bustling places. Streets were narrow and houses were built very close together. There was rubbish and dirt everywhere. Often people became ill from living in such an unhealthy environment.

Streets were not usually paved but were just dirt tracks that turned to mud in the rain. Transport was on horseback, cart or by foot. Travelling between towns was difficult and dangerous. People usually travelled in groups so they would be protected against robbers.

Edward VI and 'Bloody' Mary

Henry VIII had wanted a son because he believed that people would not trust a queen to rule properly. When he died in 1547 his son, Edward, was only nine years old. He was too young to be king, so first of all his uncle, the Duke of Somerset, and then the Duke of Northumberland governed in his name.

Edward died when he was only 15. He was very committed to the Church of England and did not want his sister, Mary, a very devout Catholic, to become queen. Before he died, Edward said that Lady Jane Grey, a distant cousin, should become queen but Mary's claim was stronger. After only nine days as queen, Lady Jane Grey was imprisoned and beheaded.

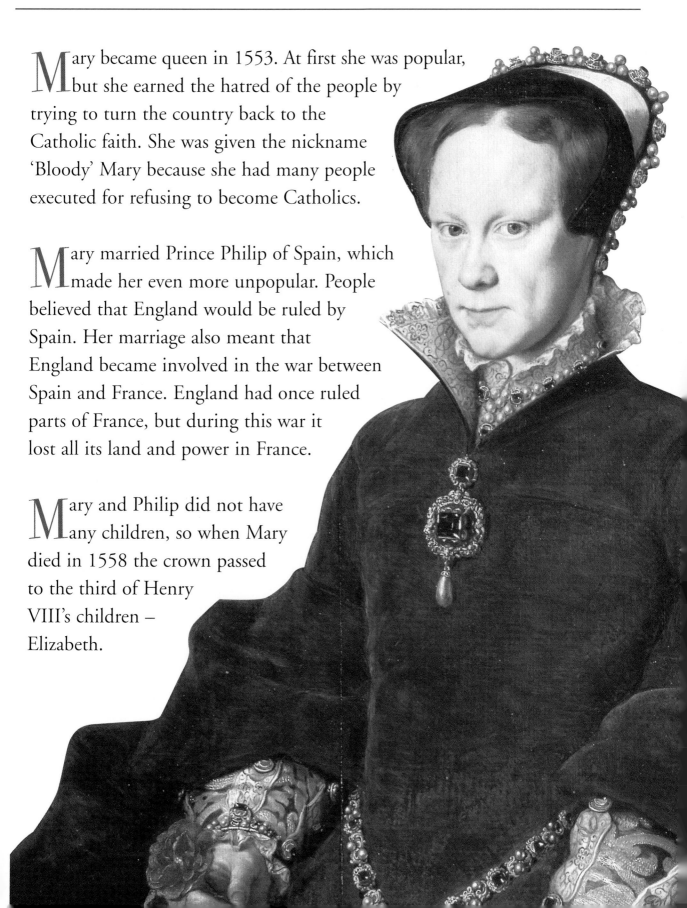

Mary became queen in 1553. At first she was popular, but she earned the hatred of the people by trying to turn the country back to the Catholic faith. She was given the nickname 'Bloody' Mary because she had many people executed for refusing to become Catholics.

Mary married Prince Philip of Spain, which made her even more unpopular. People believed that England would be ruled by Spain. Her marriage also meant that England became involved in the war between Spain and France. England had once ruled parts of France, but during this war it lost all its land and power in France.

Mary and Philip did not have many children, so when Mary died in 1558 the crown passed to the third of Henry VIII's children – Elizabeth.

Catholics and Protestants

When Henry VIII broke away from the Catholic Church in 1532 he did it mainly so he could divorce Katherine of Aragon. However, the changes to religion in England were part of a whole movement throughout Europe called the 'Reformation'.

The Reformation was started in Germany by a man called Martin Luther. He and others tried to make changes to the Catholic Church. Their attempts failed and Protestant ('protesting') Churches were set up. The Church of England was one of these Churches.

Henry made many changes to the Church in England after he became its leader. He took the great wealth of the Church for himself. He passed Acts of Parliament to 'dissolve' or get rid of the Church's monasteries. Nearly all the monastery buildings in England were destroyed.

Protestants believed in a much simpler form of worship than Catholics. During Edward VI's reign many of the statues, pictures and decorated altars in churches were destroyed. Other changes were better. Priests were allowed to marry and laws were passed saying that churches had to use a Prayer Book and a Bible in English rather than Latin so more people could understand them.

When Mary became queen she tried to turn England back into a Catholic country. She sacked, imprisoned or executed the Protestant clergy. She brought in 'heresy' laws, which meant people could be punished by death if they refused to follow the Catholic religion.

During the Tudor period thousands of people died for the sake of religion. Sometimes they were executed, at other times people were killed during the fighting over religious beliefs.

Elizabeth I and her Court

Although in the past people had believed that a woman could not rule the country as well as a man, Elizabeth became a popular queen. She earned the nickname 'Good Queen Bess'. Elizabeth was a Protestant and turned the country back to the Church of England. However, she tried to stop the arguments between the Protestants and the Catholics peacefully, unlike her sister, Mary.

Elizabeth was not rich. Her father, Henry VIII, had spent a lot of money on foreign wars and so Elizabeth tried hard to avoid war. Even though Elizabeth was not rich she enjoyed a luxurious lifestyle. She liked to ride and hunt and wear fashionable clothes.

Elizabeth's court, that is, the people who helped the Queen in her duties and entertained her, was full of clever and elegant people. During the summer months the court would leave the palace in London and travel around the country, staying at the homes of rich nobles. This was called the 'Royal Progress'. She travelled in a long procession with 400 carts. The Queen saved money because for those months of the tour the entire court was fed and entertained at the expense of the nobles whose homes were visited!

Elizabeth never married. Many men had wanted to marry her but she could not choose between them. She died without having had any children. She was the last Tudor ruler.

Exploration and Colonies

SIR WALTER RALEIGH OBT: 1618

During the Tudor period many men set out to explore the world. Sir Francis Drake and Sir Walter Raleigh are the most famous of these explorers. Drake sailed around the world between 1577 and 1580 and Raleigh explored America. He also took people there to live in new settlements or 'colonies'. Many other European countries like Spain, France and Holland also had colonies.

Throughout the Tudor and Stuart periods people settled in North America. Many of the people who left Britain to live in what became known as the 'New World' of America went because they were Protestants who did not agree with the Church of England.

The 'Pilgrim Fathers' is the name given to just such a group of people who sailed to America on a ship called

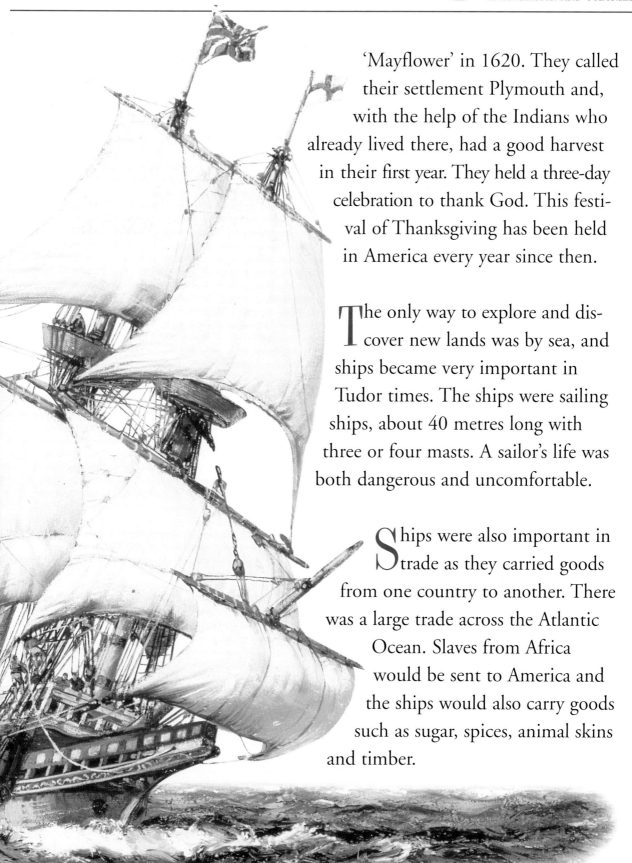

'Mayflower' in 1620. They called their settlement Plymouth and, with the help of the Indians who already lived there, had a good harvest in their first year. They held a three-day celebration to thank God. This festival of Thanksgiving has been held in America every year since then.

The only way to explore and discover new lands was by sea, and ships became very important in Tudor times. The ships were sailing ships, about 40 metres long with three or four masts. A sailor's life was both dangerous and uncomfortable.

Ships were also important in trade as they carried goods from one country to another. There was a large trade across the Atlantic Ocean. Slaves from Africa would be sent to America and the ships would also carry goods such as sugar, spices, animal skins and timber.

The Spanish Armada

Queen Elizabeth tried to avoid wars but for much of her reign England was quarrelling with Spain. Philip II of Spain, who had been married to Elizabeth's sister Mary, was still alive. He wanted to get rid of Elizabeth and make England a Catholic country again.

There were also problems at sea and in the colonies. Sailors like Sir Francis Drake attacked Spanish ports in the colonies or ships carrying treasure to other countries and stole the wealth. The Spanish thought of such men as pirates but the English thought they were heroes and Elizabeth encouraged them because they brought the treasure back to her.

Philip II decided to attack England. In 1588 a huge fleet, or 'Armada', of 130 Spanish ships set sail for England. The Armada soon ran into problems, though. They sailed into a storm and lost many of their supplies, but worse was to come.

The English had heard that Spain planned to attack them and were prepared. They had organized their own large fleet to attack the Armada. On land a system of fire beacons was set up to warn of the Armada's approach and men were ready to defend the country. However, the Spanish never landed in England. They were defeated at sea.

The English fleet included expert sailors like Sir Francis Drake. While the Armada was anchored at Calais in France, the English sent eight fire ships towards it. The Spanish ships, made of wood like all ships of the time, cut their anchors and fled so they would not be set alight. The English fleet then attacked them. To escape, the Armada had to travel around the north coast of Scotland. Terrible storms on the journey home destroyed many of the Spanish ships. Only 60 ships managed to return to Spain.

King James and the Gunpowder Plot

Elizabeth had no children and the person with the strongest claim to the throne was James VI – King of Scotland. He was the son of Mary, Queen of Scots. Mary was a Catholic and many English Catholics had plotted to make her queen instead of Elizabeth. Elizabeth had Mary executed in 1587 after a letter was found proving that Mary had been part of one of those plots.

James was of the house of Stuart and when he became King James I of England he united the thrones of Scotland and England.

Unlike his mother, James was a Protestant and was happy to be the head of the Church of England. James would not let Catholics worship as they wished. In 1605 a group of Catholics, led by Robert Catesby, plotted to blow up the Houses of Parliament when King James was there. Guy Fawkes, one of the men involved in the plot, was discovered in the cellars of the Houses of Parliament with several barrels of gunpowder. He was tortured, but did not reveal the names of the other men involved. However, they were all eventually caught and executed.

James was not a very popular king. He spent a lot of money, even though he did not have very much. When his money ran out he forced banks to lend him more and he increased taxes. He also angered Members of Parliament by insisting that he had a 'divine right', that is a right from God, to rule the country as he pleased.

King James was very interested in all aspects of religion and he ordered a new translation of the Bible into English. Today it is the most widely read book in the English language.

Shakespeare and the Theatre

During Queen Elizabeth's reign visiting the theatre became a popular pastime. Before 1572 actors used to travel from town to town and perform from the backs of wagons rather than theatres. They were not respected and were seen as little more than beggars. In 1572 a new law meant that all groups of actors had to hold a special licence. Soon after this, in 1576, the actor James Burbage built England's first public theatre. Until the reign of Charles II all actors were male; boys played the women's parts.

Many theatres were built in the late 1500s and this meant that there was a demand for new plays. There were many great dramatists – people who wrote plays – during the Elizabethan

and Stuart periods. The greatest of all these was William Shakespeare. Shakespeare wrote about 37 plays. Some were tragedies like Romeo and Juliet and Macbeth; others were comedies like A Midsummer Night's Dream and Twelfth Night. He also wrote some history plays, often based on the lives of English kings like Richard III and Henry V. His plays were very popular at the time. Both Queen Elizabeth and King James enjoyed watching his plays. Today he is thought to be the greatest English playwright ever.

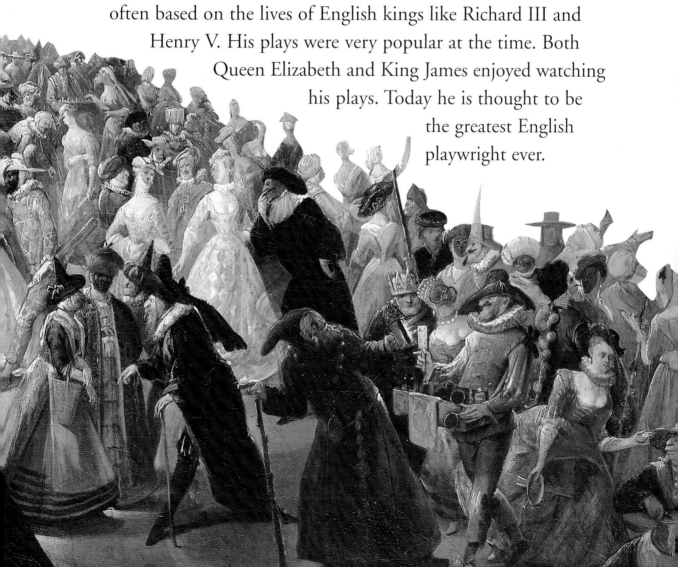

Charles I and the Civil War

Like James I, Charles I believed in the 'divine right' of kings to rule the country as they pleased. During his reign he had many arguments with Parliament over how the country should be run.

Most of the quarrels with Parliament were about money. Charles did not have enough money to pay for his wars against Austria and Spain. He forced rich people to lend him money and raised taxes. Parliament did not agree with this. Angry that Parliament seemed to be telling him what to do, Charles took all its power away and ruled the country alone for over 10 years.

During this time Charles had to face problems over religion in Scotland. Most people in Scotland were Presbyterian, a stricter form of Protestantism than the Church of England. Charles insisted that they had to use the English Prayer Book. When the Scots refused to do this Charles brought in his army to force them, but it was defeated. He later planned to attack the Scots again. Once again the Scots won, and this time they captured part of northern England.

Charles needed more money to carry on fighting the Scots, so he recalled Parliament and asked for their help. Parliament took away much of Charles' control of the country. Charles tried to show that he was in control and sent soldiers into the House of Commons to arrest the MPs' leaders. This was against the law. Riots broke out in London and Charles fled.

This was the beginning of the Civil War. On one side were the Royalists, sometimes called 'Cavaliers', who supported Charles and the idea of a monarchy. On the other side were the 'Roundheads' who supported Parliament. The Roundheads were led by Oliver Cromwell. Cromwell and his army finally beat the king's soldiers.

Charles was captured and beheaded in 1649.

The Commonwealth

Without a king the country became a 'republic' or 'commonwealth'. It was ruled by a Parliament called the 'Long Parliament'. The men who belonged to this Parliament tried to run the country, but Oliver Cromwell became very powerful. Cromwell and Parliament quarrelled so he closed it down and brought in a new Parliament made up of very religious men who would support him. This Parliament was nicknamed the 'Barebones Parliament' after one of its members, Praisegod Barebones.

This Parliament also failed to govern the country well and eventually Oliver Cromwell was made 'Lord Protector'. This meant that he had the power to rule the country as if he was a king. In fact, although he refused, Parliament suggested that he should be king.

Living in the Commonwealth was very different for most ordinary people. Cromwell and the Parliament were 'Puritans', another form of Protestantism, who believed in a simple way of life. They didn't like fancy clothes, theatre, singing, dancing, drinking, or games. There were laws and rules against all these things. In fact, although it was never used, the penalty for swearing was death!

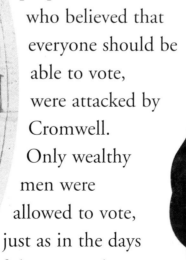

Many people believed that the Commonwealth would bring more equality for poor people and that they might be able to choose who belonged to the Parliament, but this did not happen. In fact, a group of people called the 'Levellers', who believed that everyone should be able to vote, were attacked by Cromwell. Only wealthy men were allowed to vote, just as in the days of the monarchy. People were also unhappy that the army was involved in the government.

Charles II and the Restoration

When Oliver Cromwell died in 1659 his son, Richard, became Lord Protector. However, he was a weak man and the army took away his title and power. They decided that Charles I's son should return and become king. This was known as the 'Restoration'.

Charles II's Parliament brought in laws which stopped Puritans from having government jobs and from following any other church service than that of the Church of England.

Charles II also had quarrels with Parliament. His biggest quarrel was over a secret treaty with France. This treaty gave Charles money and help in his war against Holland. In return, the King promised that Catholics could have the freedom to worship as they pleased. Parliament did not like this so they passed the 'Test Act' which meant that everyone who worked for the government had to swear that they were Protestant.

Charles' brother, James, was Catholic and Parliament was worried that if Charles II died James would become king, turning England back into a Catholic country. They tried to pass an Act to make

sure this did not happen. Charles, like his father before him, went to Parliament and dismissed it. But this Charles was able to do without Parliament because he had been given a large amount of money by Louis XIV, the King of France.

The Restoration not only brought back the monarchy but also the lifestyle that had gone with it. All the things that had been banned under Oliver Cromwell and the Commonwealth were now allowed again. Clothing became more colourful, the theatres were reopened and many new plays were written and performed. Comedies were very popular and, for the first time, women were allowed to act on stage.

37

Plague and Fire

In 1665 plague broke out in London. The Puritans believed that it was God's punishment on Charles II for his wicked lifestyle.

Plague was carried by the fleas that live on rats and the crowded and dirty streets of London meant that it spread quickly. There was no cure and about 100,000 Londoners died.

The people of London tried very hard to stop the spread of plague. The victims' bodies were buried quickly after death in huge plague pits at the edge of the city. They were collected at night by men who drove through the streets with carts calling, 'Bring out your

dead'. Doctors wore leather clothing stuffed with herbs in the belief it would protect them. Rich people, including the King, fled to the country-side to escape the infection. However, the usual way of dealing with it was to seal up the houses of those with plague, mark the door with a cross and leave the people inside to die.

The following year a second disaster struck London. On 2 September, 1666, a fire started in a baker's house in Pudding Lane. The streets of London were very narrow and the buildings were made of wood, many with roofs thatched with straw. The fire spread quickly and for several days it was out of control. It was finally stopped by blowing up several houses in the fire's path, making a gap that the fire could not cross.

Nine people died in the fire and more than 10,000 houses and nearly 100 churches were destroyed.

James II and William and Mary

Charles had many children by other women, but none by his wife Queen Catherine, so when he died in 1885 his brother, James, became king.

James II tried to turn England back into a Catholic country, which was very unpopular. When leading churchmen refused to help James, he had them arrested and put on trial. They were found not guilty, but this had made James even more unpopular.

The Duke of Monmouth, one of Charles II's illegitimate children, led a revolt against James soon after he became king. Monmouth's army was defeated and he and 300 of his followers were executed.

James' daughter, Mary, was a Protestant. She was married to William of Orange, the Dutch King. In 1688 some leading noblemen invited William and Mary to come to England and help get rid of the Catholic James. When William and his army landed in Devon he was welcomed by the people on his journey to London. James fled to France and William and Mary were crowned as joint rulers. This became known as the 'Glorious Revolution'.

William and Mary agreed to a 'Declaration of Rights' that gave Parliament more power and stopped any Catholic from becoming monarch.

Their reign was relatively peaceful but they did have one serious threat to their position. The French sent soldiers to help the Irish Catholics fight to restore James II. William defeated them at the Battle of the Boyne in 1689.

Anne and the Birth of Great Britain

Mary died in 1694 and William died in 1702. They had no children and so Mary's sister, Anne, became queen.

During Anne's reign Britain became a powerful nation in Europe. England won wars against both France and Spain.

There were also great developments in science, literature and art at this time. Writers such as Jonathan Swift and Alexander Pope published important books and pamphlets dealing with topical issues. Thomas Newcomen invented the steam engine. Christopher Wren, a scientist and architect, completed his most famous building, St Paul's Cathedral.

One of the most important things to happen while Anne was queen was the Union of Scotland with England and Wales. From 1707 Anne ruled what was called the United Kingdom of Great Britain.

Henry VIII had taken over Wales in 1536 and James I had united the thrones of Scotland and England in 1603. Scotland retained its own Parliament but by the beginning of the eighteenth century most Scots had begun to realize that it was impossible for them to be independent. They were in need of money and wanted to be able to trade freely with England. The 'Act of Union' was passed in 1707 and the two Parliaments became one.

A flag was designed to reflect the Union. The first British Union Flag, or Union Jack, had the flags of Wales, Scotland and England combined.

Anne had 17 children, all of whom died. When she died the crown passed to her cousin, George of Hanover.

Places to Visit

Shakespeare's Globe Theatre – reconstruction of Shakespeare's Globe Theatre, includes a museum and stages plays. Shakespeare's Globe, New Globe Walk, London, SE1 9DT. Telephone: 0171 902 1400.

Houses of Parliament – contains many paintings and documents, including Charles I's death warrant. House of Commons, London, SW1A 0AA. Telephone: 0171 219 4272.

Pudding Lane – small plaque marks site of start of Great Fire of London. London, EC3

Tower of London – where many of state prisoners were held. Also includes displays of armoury and weapons of the period. HM Tower of London, London, EC3N 4AB. Telephone: 0171 709 0765.

National Portrait Gallery – portraits of many of the monarchs and other people of the time. The National Portrait Gallery, 2 St Martins Place, London, WC2H 0HE. Telephone: 0171 306 0055.

National Maritime Museum – paintings of ships and sea battles. Displays of maps, charts, globes and navigational instruments. The National Maritime Museum, Park Row, Greenwich, London, SE10 9NF. Telephone: 0181 858 4422.

Old Royal Observatory – displays of many scientific explorations and discoveries. Old Royal Observatory, Park Row, Greenwich, London, SE10 9NF. Telephone: 0181 858 4422.

Hampton Court – home of Cardinal Wolsley, Henry VIII's adviser, later owed by Henry. Has a famous Maze. Hampton Court Palace, Surrey, KT8 9AU. Telephone: 0181 781 9500.

The Mary Rose - Henry VIII's ship that sank in Portsmouth Harbour and was recovered in 1982. HM Dockyard, Mary Rose Trust, No. 5 The Boathouse,

College Road, Portsmouth, PO33 3PX. Telephone: 01705 812931.

Ham House – building, furnishing and decorations of the period. Near Richmond. Telephone: 0181 332 6644

Hatfield House – paintings and furnishings of the period. Hatfield House, Hertfordshire, AL9 5NQ. Telephone: 01707 262823.

Stratford-upon-Avon – many Elizabethan timber buildings, including Shakespeare's house. The Shakespeare Centre, Henley Street, Stratford-upon-Avon, CV37 6QW. Telephone: 01789 204016.

Blenheim Palace – home of Duke of Marlborough. Good example of Stuart architecture and furnishings. Blenheim Palace, Woodstock, Oxfordshire, OX20 1PX. Telephone: 01993 811325.

Speke Hall – Tudor House. National Trust, Speke Hall, The Walk, Speke, Liverpool, L24 1XD. Telephone: 0151 427 7231.

Holyrood Palace – home of Mary, Queen of Scots. The Palace Of Holyrood House, Edinburgh, EH8 8DX. Telephone: 0131 556 1096.

Erddig – Stuart house with many original features. The National Trust, Erddig, Wrexham, LL13 0YT. Telephone: 01978 355314.

Picture Credits